Do Goldfish Play the Violin?

David Henry Wilson

Illustrated by Patricia Drew

Piccolo Books

First published 1985 by J. M. Dent & Sons Ltd.
This Piccolo edition published 1987 by Pan Books Ltd,
Cavaye Place, London SW10 9PG
9 8 7 6 5 4 3 2 1
Text © David Henry Wilson 1985
Illustrations © Patricia Drew 1985
ISBN 0 330 29594 2

Printed and bound in Great Britain by
Collins, Glasgow

For my brother Peter,
to read to Robin and Ian

Contents

1 Monday Morning 1

2 Yellow and Purple 9

3 A Note in the Wind 18

4 A Present for Timothy 28

5 A Frightening Experience 37

6 Do Goldfish Play the Violin? 46

7 The Battleaxe 56

8 How to Stop Paying Bills 66

9 The Magician 76

10 The Robbers 86

11 Mr Blooming 96

12 Cold Nativity 107

Monday Morning

Jeremy James watched in amazement as his bowl of cornflakes slid across the table.

Swish, crash, tinkle, smash, wah!

These were the sounds made by the breakfast things as they all fell from the table to the floor – except 'wah!' which was the sound made by Christopher as the cornflake packet landed on his head.

The breakfast things had fallen to the floor because of Jennifer's right hand, right leg, and left leg. Her right hand had caught hold of the table cloth, and her right leg and left leg had carried her across the room while she was still holding the cloth. And so down came the cloth and cornflakes and all.

'Oh, you naughty girl,' said Jeremy James.

'Oh, you naughty, naughty girl!' cried Mummy, and gave Jennifer a smack on the bottom. Jennifer smiled sweetly, pointed to the collection of cups and cornflakes, milk and marmalade, bowls and butter all over the floor, and said, 'Mess!'

Mummy set to work cleaning up the mess, Jeremy James kissed Christopher's head better, and Daddy came downstairs with his razor in his hand and a cut on his chin.

'What happened?' he asked.

'Jennifer pulled the cloth off,' said Mummy.

'You naughty girl,' said Daddy.

'Nor-ty,' said Jennifer. 'Nor-ty.'

The twins were a menace. Now that they could walk, they were everywhere. Daddy had put a gate at the top of the stairs to make sure they didn't fall down. Only Daddy had forgotten about the gate one night, and *he* had fallen down. He had also bought a huge playpen to keep them fenced in, but they couldn't be fenced in all the time, and it was during the unfenced-in time that they were a menace. Jennifer was more of a menace than Christopher. She now waddled over to have a look at him.

'Wiffer cwy,' she said.

'Of course he's crying,' said Jeremy James. 'He got hit on the head by the cornflakes.'

Jennifer lifted the packet of cornflakes and smacked it hard. 'Nor-ty corflay!' she said, and laughed.

Daddy helped Mummy with the tidying, until he cut his finger on a broken saucer and went upstairs to get some plaster.

'Daddy blood!' said Jennifer.

'And it's your fault,' said Jeremy James.

'Nor-ty Jeffer,' said Jennifer.

'Any idea where the plaster is?' came Daddy's voice from upstairs.

'In the medicine cupboard,' called Mummy.

By the time Daddy had come downstairs again, with a plaster on his chin and on his finger, Mummy had set the breakfast table, the twins were in the playpen, and Jeremy James was halfway through his toast and marmalade.

'What a start to the week!' said Daddy. 'Typical Monday morning.'

But worse was to follow. Daddy had to go out, and after breakfast Jeremy James wandered into his study to watch him getting things ready. It was always interesting to watch Daddy get things ready. First he had to find his papers, then his pen, his wallet, his cheque book, his what's-a-name (he could *never* find his what's-a-name), and finally his brief case. It was Jeremy James who found the brief case, which had somehow got wedged between the filing cabinet and the bookcase.

'Thanks, Jeremy James,' said Daddy. 'I really must get this place tidied up. Right, now we're all set. Where are the car keys?'

And that was when the trouble really started. They were not on the desk, they were not on the

key hook, and they were not in his jacket pocket.

'Have you looked in your overcoat?' asked Mummy.

Daddy hadn't looked in his overcoat. But when he did look in his overcoat, there were no car keys.

'Have you looked in your trousers?' asked Jeremy James.

Daddy put his hands in his trouser pockets. No car keys.

Daddy went into his study, shouted

'Yaaaaaahgrrrrrraaaaaah!' very loudly, and hurled a bunch of papers all over the room. But even that didn't bring the keys out of hiding.

'I can't understand it!' Daddy howled. 'I had them yesterday! Things just disappear in this house.'

'They don't disappear,' said Mummy. 'You lose them. You should keep things tidier.'

'I don't lose them,' said Daddy. 'They move around.'

It occurred to Jeremy James that the keys might have moved around with Daddy.

'They might be in the medicine cupboard,' he suggested.

'Not likely,' said Daddy. 'Plaster goes in the medicine cupboard. And medicine.'

'And keys,' said Mummy, 'go on the key hook.'

Daddy went upstairs. The keys were not in the medicine cupboard.

'Have you looked in your other jackets and trousers?' asked Mummy.

While Mummy and Daddy searched jackets and trousers, Jeremy James searched Daddy's study again, but the keys had not fallen down between the filing cabinet and the bookcase, or under Daddy's desk, or inside his typewriter, or into his wastepaper basket. Nor had they been found in the other jackets and trousers.

'Just stop and think,' said Mummy. 'When did you have them last?'

Daddy stopped and thought. 'Yesterday, when I washed the car,' he said.

'And where did you put them?' asked Mummy.

'If I knew where I'd put them,' said Daddy, 'I'd know where to find them.'

'I know where Daddy sometimes puts the car keys,' said Jeremy James.

'Where?' asked Daddy.

'In the car,' said Jeremy James.

'Aha!' said Daddy. 'I didn't think of that.'

Out went Daddy to look in the car. And back came Daddy from looking in the car. The car was locked, and there were no keys in it.

'Well, you'll just have to take the spare keys,' said Mummy.

'I can't,' said Daddy.

'Why not?' asked Mummy.

'They're lost,' said Daddy.

Jeremy James wandered into the living room. That had been searched three or four times but had proved as keyless as all the other rooms. The keys had vanished and it looked as if they would never be unvanished.

'Jem Jem!' said Jennifer from the playpen.

'Hello,' said Jeremy James. 'You haven't seen Daddy's keys, have you?'

'Keys!' said Jennifer, and shook her hand in the air. In her hand was something small and shiny and rattly.

Jeremy James went a little closer.

'What have you got?' he asked.

Jennifer smiled.

'Show me,' said Jeremy James.

Jennifer smiled again and waddled to the other side of the playpen.

'Have you got Daddy's keys?' asked Jeremy James.

'Keys!' said Jennifer.

Jeremy James marched to the other side of the playpen.

Jennifer smiled.

'Jem Jem!' she said, and threw the small, shiny, rattly something out on to the carpet. Jeremy James picked it up. It was two keys and a leather tag on a ring.

'You *are* a naughty girl!' said Jeremy James, and raced at full throttle into Daddy's study.

'Are these the keys?' he asked.

Daddy's mouth flapped open like a car bonnet.

'Where were they?' he asked.

'In the living room,' said Jeremy James.

'They couldn't have been!' said Daddy. 'I looked all over the living room!'

Jeremy James thought he'd better not

mention Jennifer. She had certainly done the finding, but she had almost certainly done the losing, too.

'They were just by the playpen,' he said – which was true because Jennifer had thrown them there.

'Well done, Jeremy James,' said Daddy. 'I must have dropped them when I was helping Mummy.'

That might have been true as well. But after Daddy had finally left, and while Mummy was washing up the breakfast things, Jeremy James asked Jennifer where she had found the keys. Jennifer smiled sweetly, and said:

'Jeffer nor-ty girl.'

It had been a typical Monday morning.

Yellow and Purple

'Look at that hair,' said Mummy.

Jeremy James tilted his head back and switched his eyes right up under his eyebrows, but he still couldn't see his hair.

'It's far too long,' said Mummy. 'He'd better have it cut.'

Mummy always cut Jeremy James's hair, but now she thought it was time he had it done properly at the barber's.

'I'm going into town this morning,' said Daddy. 'I'll take him, and he can have it cut while I'm at the library.'

An hour later, when Daddy had found his papers, pen, and the list of things he wanted to look up in the library, the two of them set off for town. Daddy took Jeremy James straight to the barber's, where he told a fat man with a moustache that he would come back for his son in an hour. The fat man nodded, and Jeremy James sat down in a chair against the wall to wait his turn.

'I shan't be long,' said Daddy, 'so just wait till I get back.'

There were two big chairs on the other side of
the room in front of mirrors, and two men were
sitting in the chairs having their hair cut. The
fat man with a moustache was seeing to one,
and a thin, pale young man was seeing to the
other. Jeremy James could see the customers'
faces in the mirrors. One of them (the fat
man's) had had nearly all his hair cut off, and
the fat man had just taken a razor to do the rest.
The other one had the strangest hair Jeremy

James had ever seen – it was yellow and purple, and some of it was standing up as stiff and straight as a brush.

A worried expression crossed Jeremy James's face. He didn't want *all* his hair cut off, so he hoped that the fat man wouldn't see to him. On the other hand, he didn't want yellow and purple hair either.

Jeremy James glanced at the man waiting in the chair next to him. He was an old man with a bald head and glasses, and he smiled at Jeremy James. Jeremy James didn't smile back. The worried look on his face was now joined by a puzzled look.

'Excuse me,' he said.

'What is it, sonny?' asked the old man kindly.

'If you've had your hair cut off,' said Jeremy James, 'why are you waiting?'

'I haven't had it cut off,' said the old man. 'And do you know why?'

'Why?' asked Jeremy James.

'Because,' said the old man, 'you can't cut off what isn't there. I lost my hair a long time ago.'

'Couldn't you find it again?' asked Jeremy James.

'I'm afraid not,' said the old man.

'I carry mine around with me,' said Jeremy James. 'On my head.'

'That's the best place to keep it,' said the old man.

Then Jeremy James again asked the old man why he was waiting, and the old man said he'd come for a shave, to get rid of the bristles on his chin.

'So you'll go to the fat man,' said Jeremy James. 'He's got the razor.'

'I expect Mr Simon will see to me, yes,' said the old man.

If the old man was going to the fat man, it meant that Jeremy James would not have all his hair cut off. That was good. But then Jeremy James would be going to the thin man, and that meant he would have yellow and purple hair. And that wasn't so good. Jeremy James began to wish that Daddy hadn't gone away.

The fat man finished balding his customer, who looked at himself in the mirror.

'Is that all right, sir?' asked the fat man.

'Yeah, OK, 's fine, OK, yeah,' said the newly bald man.

He gave the fat man some money, and Jeremy James watched as the shiny head went past him like a walking lollipop, and left the shop.

The old man next to Jeremy James got up from his chair.

'Hallo, Mr Williams,' said the fat man.

'Hallo, Frederick,' said the old man. 'It seems I've started a fashion, eh?'

They both laughed, though Jeremy James couldn't see what there was to laugh at. On the contrary, he felt more like crying than laughing. No hair in one chair, and coloured spikes in the other – it was no laughing matter at all. Maybe Daddy didn't know what they did at this barber's. Mummy often said that Daddy lived in a world of his own, so how *could* he know? If only he would come back quickly, before it was Jeremy James's turn to sit in the chair.

But Daddy didn't come back. And the yellow-and-purple man was looking at himself in the mirror.

'Very nice,' he said.

'Is it to sir's satisfaction?' asked the thin pale man.

'Yeah, very nice,' said Yellow-and-Purple. 'I like it. It's very nice. Very nice. That's what it is. Yeah.'

He gave the thin pale man some money, and Jeremy James watched as the bristly head went past him, like a walking toothbrush.

'Your turn now, son,' said the thin pale man to Jeremy James.

Jeremy James turned as pale as the thin pale man. He stood up. Yellow-and-Purple had just opened the shop door. Jeremy James looked at

the door, looked at the thin pale man, looked at the chair, and then ran as fast as he could straight past Yellow-and-Purple and out into the street.

'Come back!' shouted a voice.

Jeremy James had no intention of going back, but when he glanced behind him, he saw that the thin pale man and the yellow-and-purple man were both running after him.

'Stop him!' they shouted.

Jeremy James looked to the front again, and found himself running straight into a pair of dark blue trousers.

'Oops!' said a deep voice.

'Ouf!' said Jeremy James.

Then he was lifted high into the air until he was face to face with a silver badge on a helmet.

'Now where are you off to in such a 'urry, me lad?' asked the policeman.

With a phew and a puff and a gasp the thin pale man and Yellow-and-Purple came up to the policeman.

'No!' shouted Jeremy James. 'Go away! Go away!'

The policeman joggled him up and down in his arms.

'You're all right, sonny,' he said. 'You're quite safe wi' me. Now I wants to know what's goin' on.'

The thin pale man told the policeman that the little boy's father had left him to have his hair cut, but he had run out of the shop.

'Is that right?' asked the policeman.

Jeremy James pointed to the yellow and purple spikes.

'I don't want them. . .' he sobbed. 'I don't want to be yellow and purple.'

'I'm not surprised,' said the policeman. 'Nor would I. But you won't be like that. Did you think you were going to be like that?'

'Yes,' said Jeremy James.

The policeman laughed out loud, and the other two men laughed as well. But Jeremy James knew it wasn't funny, because if his hair was not to be yellow and purple, it was to be cut off, and that was just as bad.

'I don't. . . I don't. . .' he sobbed, 'I don't want to be balded either.'

'Balded?' said the policeman.

'By the fat man,' said Jeremy James.

'I think,' said the policeman, 'that this case is a bit more serious than we'd thought. What's yer name, son?'

'Jeremy James,' said Jeremy James.

'Right, Jeremy James,' said the policeman. 'We'd better let your Dad sort it out. Where is he?'

Jeremy James told the policeman that Daddy

was in the library, and so he and the policeman walked hand in hand up the street, left at the traffic lights, across the zebra crossing, round the corner, and into the library.

Daddy was very surprised to see a policeman come into the library with Jeremy James. He was so surprised that he dropped his pen, made a grab for it, and in so doing knocked a thick book off the table and on to the floor. Several people turned round and said, 'Sh!'

The policeman and Daddy and Jeremy James all went outside so that the policeman could explain what had happened.

'If I was you, sir,' said the policeman, 'I wouldn't leave a little lad alone in a strange place. You never know what little lads can start thinking.'

Daddy thanked the policeman who said goodbye to Jeremy James and walked away, shaking his head.

'You know what I think we should do, Jeremy James?' said Daddy. 'I think we should go home and let Mummy cut your hair as usual. Don't you?'

Jeremy James did.

A Note in the Wind

Jeremy James had gone to Richard's house to play. Round and red-faced Richard lived at No. 24, with his round and red-faced mother, his thin and pale-faced father, and his tiny wrinkled grandmother. Jeremy James liked them all except Gran, who had a funny smell and a loud voice. Richard's mother had once told Jeremy James that Gran was a little deaf. Richard said he wished he was deaf sometimes so that he couldn't hear Gran's loud voice.

It was a windy day, and the boys were in the garden playing with Richard's model glider. They threw it high in the air, and watched it swoop and swerve in the wind until it either levelled out into a perfect landing, or – more frequently – nose-dived straight into the grass. It was great fun, and they were really enjoying themselves when. . .

'Richard!'

'Oh no,' said Richard, 'it's Gran.'

'Richard!'

'I'm coming, Gran!'

'Richard!'

'I'll have to go and see what she wants,' said Richard.

Gran wanted some cigarettes. She gave Richard five pounds and said he could buy some sweets for himself and Jeremy James.

'She's quite nice really,' said Richard. 'It's just that she doesn't *seem* nice.'

Gran had also given him a letter addressed to the shop man (because otherwise he wouldn't let Richard have the cigarettes), and so Richard put the letter in one pocket, the five-pound note in the other, and set off with Jeremy James.

'I don't know why she smokes cigarettes, anyway,' said Richard. 'She's always coughing.'

'I expect that's what made her go deaf,' said Jeremy James.

'Yes, so she wouldn't hear herself coughing,' said Richard.

'And she's got a funny smell, your Gran,' said Jeremy James. 'She ought to stop smoking.'

'She does,' said Richard. 'But then she starts again.'

The playground was on the way to the shop, and so Richard and Jeremy James went for a swing and a see-saw. Then they slid on the slide and rode on the roundabout. And after that they went to the shop. When they got to the

shop, Richard pulled the letter out of one pocket, felt in the other and. . .

'It's gone!' cried Richard.

'What's gone?' asked Mr Drew, the shop man.

'The five pounds!' cried Richard. 'The five pounds has gone!'

Mr Drew had grey hair, twinkling grey eyes, and a kind heart.

'Steady on, lad,' he said. 'Don't panic. Have a good look through your pockets.'

But apart from a piece of string, a rubber band, a toffee-wrapper, a paper handkerchief, an old bus ticket, a piece of fluff, a feather, a penny piece, half a pencil and another piece of string, Richard's pockets were empty.

'What about you, Jeremy James?' asked Mr Drew. 'You sure you haven't got it?'

Jeremy James hadn't got it either.

'Well I'll tell you what to do,' said Mr Drew. 'Go back over everywhere you've been, and search carefully. It can't have gone far. I'd come with you, only I can't leave the shop, you see.'

Richard and Jeremy James went back down the street, with their noses almost scraping the pavement as they searched. Richard couldn't see very much, though, because his eyes were filled with tears.

'Gran'll kill me!' he sobbed. 'I'm not going home. I'm going to run away.'

'Maybe it's in the playground,' said Jeremy James.

Like two bloodhounds they shuffled, heads down, between the swing and the see-saw, the slide and the roundabout – but there was no five-pound note.

'It's blown away!' cried Richard. 'We'll never see it again!'

A man came by with a dog.

'Excuse me,' said Jeremy James. 'You haven't seen a five-pound note, have you?'

'I do occasionally see them,' said the man. 'Any particular one?'

'Richard's,' said Jeremy James. 'It's a blue one.'

'Ah!' said the man. 'Lost it, has he?'

'Yes,' said Jeremy James.

But the man hadn't seen it. And his dog hadn't seen it either. And a lady who came by pushing a pram hadn't seen it, and another lady with a shopping basket hadn't seen it, and the park attendant with the peaked cap and the red nose hadn't seen it. They all had a look round, but they all thought the wind must have taken it.

'And if the wind ain't took it,' said the park

attendant, 'then someone else 'as!'

'I'm never going home!' sobbed Richard. 'I'll run away to sea.'

'To see what?' asked Jeremy James.

'To sea,' said Richard. 'On a boat. Like Grandad.'

'Does your grandad live on a boat?' asked Jeremy James.

'No, he doesn't live anywhere now,' said Richard. 'He's dead. But he lived on a boat when he was alive.'

'I expect he wanted to get away from Gran's smoke,' said Jeremy James.

Since Richard couldn't go home, and since he didn't want to run away to sea just yet, Jeremy James suggested he should come and live at Jeremy James's house.

'Do you think your mummy'll mind?' asked Richard.

'No,' said Jeremy James. 'She likes children.'

And so the two boys went to Jeremy James's house.

'Oh, hello,' said Mummy, 'I thought you were both playing at Richard's house today.'

'No,' said Jeremy James, 'Richard's run away, so he's coming to live with us. Is that all right, Mummy?'

'Oh!' said Mummy. 'Well, it would be nice to

have Richard living with us, but I don't think *his* mummy'll be very pleased. Have you told her, Richard?'

'Well, no. . . not yet,' said Richard. 'But I don't think she'll mind.'

Then Mummy asked Richard why he'd run away. Richard started explaining what had happened, and Jeremy James finished explaining what had happened, because Richard began to cry again.

'I see,' said Mummy, and sat there thinking for a minute or two. Then she looked at Richard, who was still crying, and she looked at Jeremy James, who was looking at Richard crying, and she said:

'Now that's very strange. That's very strange indeed. Just wait a moment.'

She went to her handbag, opened it, and felt inside. Then she pulled out a five-pound note.

'Was it a blue one like this?'

Richard stopped crying, and both boys peered closely at the five-pound note.

'Yes, it was,' said Jeremy James.

'And did it have numbers on it like these?' asked Mummy.

'Yes, I think so,' said Richard.

'And did it have a picture of the Queen like this?' asked Mummy.

'I think so,' said Richard.

'Well that *is* a stroke of luck,' said Mummy. 'Because when I opened the front door just now, the wind blew this five-pound note straight into my hand. So it must be yours, Richard. Now I think you'd better hurry back to the shop for Gran's cigarettes, or she'll wonder where you've got to.'

Richard and Jeremy James ran all the way back to the shop.

'Ah, you found it then!' said Mr Drew.

Jeremy James explained how the wind had blown the five-pound note into Mummy's hand, and Mr Drew's eyes twinkled even more merrily than usual.

'Fancy that!' he said. 'Now I'll tell *you* something. I was sweeping the floor just now, and under the counter I found two pound coins and a 50p piece. And I happen to know, Jeremy James, that they all belong to your mother, who must have dropped them when she came in yesterday. Would you give them to her, please, and tell her they're from me.'

Jeremy James took the three coins, and Richard bought the cigarettes and sweets and put the change carefully in his pocket.

'Make sure you don't lose it,' said Mr Drew.

'I won't,' said Richard and Jeremy James together.

When the two boys got back to Richard's house, Gran was fast asleep, so she couldn't have noticed how long they'd been.

'She's always asleep,' said Richard.

'I expect the smoke gets in her eyes,' said Jeremy James.

At teatime, Jeremy James went home and gave the money to Mummy. She was quite surprised to get it, but when Jeremy James told her what Mr Drew had said, she nodded and smiled.

'We all seem to be losing our money,' she said.

'*And* finding it,' said Jeremy James.

'That's right,' said Mummy. 'We *are* lucky.'

And her eyes were twinkling just like Mr Drew's.

A Present from Timothy

'No, I don't want to invite *him*,' said Jeremy James. 'He always spoils everything.'

'I know,' said Mummy, 'but we don't want to offend the Smyth-Fortescues.'

Him was Timothy, who lived next door, was a year older than Jeremy James, and knew everything about everything.

'I don't mind offending the Smile-Forty-queues,' said Jeremy James.

'You'll have to invite him all the same,' said Mummy.

The invitation was to Jeremy James's birthday party, and inviting Timothy would be like asking an elephant to share your glass of lemonade. What was shared with Timothy became Timothy's.

'Go round and tell him now,' said Mummy.

'Do I have to?' moaned Jeremy James, trying to disappear into the floor.

'Yes,' said Mummy.

Mrs Smyth-Fortescue opened the door when Jeremy James rang to deliver the invitation.

'Oh, how lovely!' she said. 'He loves parties.'

'But if he's doing something else,' said Jeremy James, 'I'll be very pleased.'

'No, of course he isn't. Are you, dear?'

'No,' said Timothy. 'I don't mind coming to your party, though it won't be as good as mine.'

'Thank you so much, Jeremy,' said Mrs Smyth-Fortescue, who never remembered to call him Jeremy James. 'Timothy will be there, don't worry.'

It was because Timothy would be there that Jeremy James did worry, but at least it would mean an extra present.

'Don't forget my present,' he said to Timothy.

'Your presents won't be as good as mine,' said Timothy.

The birthday began with a red pedal-car from Mummy and Daddy, which had a horn that really hooted and lights that really lit. Jeremy James spent most of the morning in his pedal-car, but as it was raining outside, he couldn't give it a proper speed-test. Instead he tested the steering – round and sometimes into the furniture – the lights, and especially the horn. For some reason Daddy told Mummy the horn had been a mistake, but Jeremy James couldn't find anything wrong with it.

Other presents included a football from the

twins, and a big box of games from Uncle Jack, Aunt Janet and cousin Melissa. These were morning presents from the family. Next there would be afternoon presents from the friends.

One by one they arrived. Little Trevor came with a bag of sweets (he'd tried them and said they were very nice), fat Richard brought a model glider, and there were books and toys and games which Jeremy James laid out on the sideboard so that everyone could see what he'd got.

But the most interesting present was Timothy's. At first Timothy wouldn't even give it to him.

'You're too young,' he said. 'My mummy really bought it for me, and I don't think you should have it.'

'Then why's it wrapped in birthday paper?' asked Jeremy James.

Mummy came by at that moment, and noticed that not only was it wrapped in birthday paper, but it also had Jeremy James's name on it.

Timothy pulled a grumpy face, and thrust out the packet without even looking at Jeremy James.

'There you are,' he said. 'But it's not really for little kids like you.'

Jeremy James opened the packet. Inside the wrapping paper was a white box which was small, but quite heavy. Jeremy James opened the white box, and found something that looked like a pocket-knife but wasn't.

'It's a torch,' said Timothy, 'and it's got a compass and a magnifying glass and a screwdriver and a bottle-opener and a ruler and. . . well, it's really for me. I should have had it, not you.'

Jeremy James loved the torch. It was his second-best present after the pedal-car, and he put it right at the front of his pile of things on the sideboard. The other children liked it, too, and when they'd had a sit in the pedal-car and had flashed the lights and honked the horn, most of them wanted to look through the magnifying glass, switch the torch on and off, and turn the compass around. Timothy stayed beside it to show everyone how it worked, and to make sure they knew it came from him. He wasn't interested in the pedal-car anyway, because he had a bigger one with a horn and lights and a lift-up bonnet and a slide-over roof.

The party was a great success. The crisps and crackers, buns and biscuits, jam tarts and jellies all disappeared without leaving a trace, and nobody was sick. There were no tears in any of the games, and everybody won a prize. Timothy didn't cheat, and didn't even tell Jeremy James that his own party had been better. In fact, Timothy hardly said a word all afternoon, which was as strange as a monkey not eating bananas.

When at last it was time for everyone to leave, Mummy gave them all a packet of sweets and a little game to take home with them. Then, as the first goodbyes were being said, Jeremy James saw something. To be more precise, Jeremy James didn't see something. What he didn't see was his torch-compass-magnifying glass.

'Where's my torch?' he cried.

Mummy came to have a look. Then Daddy came to have a look. And then all the children came to have a look. And what they all looked at was the space where the torch had been and now was not.

'It's gone,' said Daddy.

'Maybe it's fallen behind the sideboard,' said Mummy.

But it hadn't.

'Maybe it's fallen into Timothy's pocket,' said Jeremy James.

'Yes,' said fat Richard, 'I bet Timothy's got it.'

'No I haven't!' said Timothy, going as red as a jam tart. 'I haven't got it! I haven't!'

'Of course you haven't,' said Mummy quickly. 'You mustn't say things like that, Jeremy James.'

'I bet he has, though,' said Jeremy James to Richard.

Mummy now called the children together and told them they were going to play one last game.

'I want you to stand round the sideboard,' she said, 'and when I tell you to, close your eyes and wish very hard that the torch comes back.

Will you do that?'

'Yes!' said a dozen voices.

Mummy placed the children in front of the sideboard, and she got Timothy to stand right by the spot where the torch had been.

'Now if the torch doesn't come back,' said Mummy, 'we'll all empty our pockets, just in case the torch accidentally fell into one. Right?'

'Yes!' said a dozen voices.

'Good,' said Mummy. 'Now then, close your eyes and don't open them till I tell you to. Otherwise you'll break the magic spell. And if anyone *does* open his eyes, he'll lose his prizes and his sweets and his present.'

A dozen pairs of eyes were tightly closed.

'Now wish with all your might that the torch comes back.'

There was a rich and wishy silence as a dozen children (minus one) willed the torch back on to the sideboard. Jeremy James thought he heard a movement next to him. He opened his eyes to tiny slits, and saw Timothy stepping back from the sideboard.

'You can open your eyes now,' said Mummy.

The eyes opened. Then the mouths opened as well, for there on the sideboard was the torch.

'Well done, everybody,' said Mummy.

'Sheer magic!' said Daddy.

'Timothy moved,' said Jeremy James.

'No, I didn't,' said Timothy.

'Did anybody see Timothy move?' asked Mummy.

Jeremy James did some quick thinking. He *had* seen Timothy move, but in order to see him, he'd had to open his eyes, and Mummy had said that anyone opening his eyes would lose prizes, sweets and present. Or had she perhaps even said presents? Jeremy James kept quiet. So did fat Richard and little Trevor.

'Mummy,' said Jeremy James, when everyone had gone home. 'Timothy did move.'

'Yes, I know,' said Mummy.

'Then he should have lost his prizes and sweets,' said Jeremy James.

'But you,' said Mummy, 'opened your eyes, didn't you?'

'Um. . . yes,' said Jeremy James.

'So you,' said Mummy, 'should have lost your prizes and sweets *and* presents.'

'Hmmph,' said Jeremy James, and went to look at his car through the magnifying glass.

A Frightening Experience

Daddy and Jeremy James were going fishing. Fishing was Daddy's latest hobby, and he said it was much more enjoyable than football, television, and paying bills. As Jeremy James had never been fishing, Mummy suggested he should go with Daddy, and as Jeremy James was not doing anything special that afternoon, he and Daddy duly set off for the river. Daddy was carrying a big bag and had his fishing rod slung over his shoulder like a nervous rifle. Over Jeremy James's shoulder was a net, and he was carrying a tin that was full of squiggly maggots.

'What are the maggots for?' asked Jeremy James.

'Bait,' said Daddy.

'What's bait?' asked Jeremy James.

'We put the maggot on the hook,' said Daddy, 'then the fish tries to eat the maggot and gets caught on the hook.'

Jeremy James thought Daddy should put chocolate or liquorice-all-sorts on the hook, but

Daddy said fish preferred maggots.

Jeremy James thought fish must be very silly creatures, and he felt sorry for the maggots.

'This looks a good spot,' said Daddy, when they had reached the river. 'Let's try here.'

He took two folding stools out of the bag and set them on the ground. Then he took a maggot out of the tin and fixed it on the hook of his fishing line.

'Doesn't that hurt?' asked Jeremy James.

'Ouch!' said Daddy, sticking the hook in his thumb. 'Yes, it does!'

'I meant the maggot,' said Jeremy James.

Daddy told Jeremy James to stand clear, and with a swing and a heave he threw the maggot, hook and line far out into the water where they landed with a plop, and disappeared from view.

'Now,' said Daddy, 'you see the red-and-white float bobbing up and down?'

'Yes,' said Jeremy James.

'Well, if it moves around, we've got a bite, and if it goes under the water, we've got a fish. So watch carefully.'

They both sat down on the folding stools and watched the red-and-white float. It bobbed gently up and down, but it didn't move around and it didn't go under the water.

'How long will it be?' asked Jeremy James.

'I don't know,' said Daddy. 'Fish are a bit

like trains – you never know how long they'll keep you waiting.'

Daddy and Jeremy James waited a long time. But the red-and-white float still didn't move around and still didn't go under the water.

'Maybe the maggot's run away,' said Jeremy James.

'Or gone for a swim,' said Daddy.

He wound the line in, and the float came up out of the water, followed by an empty, maggot-less hook.

Three times Daddy threw hooked maggots into the water, three times they waited and watched, and three times the hook came back empty.

'Can't even catch a maggot!' grumbled Daddy.

Jeremy James had decided that fishing was the silliest, boringest, pointlessest game he'd ever played when suddenly...

'We've got a bite!' said Daddy.

Jeremy James fixed his eyes on the red-and-white float, and sure enough it was ducking and jerking in all directions. A moment later, under it went.

'Got you!' said Daddy, and began to wind in the line. 'Quite a big one, too, from the way it's pulling.'

Jeremy James watched as the float came up out of the water.

'Now get the net ready, Jeremy James,' said Daddy, 'and as soon as the fish comes near, see if you can catch it in the net.'

Out came the fish. It *was* a big one, and it was flashing silver in the sun as it writhed and wriggled on the hook. Nearer and nearer it came, and Jeremy James reached out the net to catch it. And that was the moment when a terrible thing happened. Jeremy James reached out too far, his foot slipped on a patch of mud, and as the fish came from water to bank, so Jeremy James went from bank to water. There was a loud splash as he tumbled headfirst into a cold, swirling wetness that closed over his head with a loud gurgling roar.

The water bellowed into his ears and blocked his nose and blurred his eyes. He kicked his legs and flailed his arms, trying to keep it away.

Suddenly his head was above the water, and he just had time to see the green bank and the trees and fields before once more he was sucked down, and the roaring filled his head again. He couldn't breathe. There was blackness all around him. He kicked and flailed.

Up he rose above the water. He gasped for air, crying as the air came into him. 'Daddy!' he shouted. But then his mouth filled with water

again as the river pulled him down. He just saw
a shape moving towards him before he went
under, falling into rushing darkness, flashing
lights, and a coldness that now made him too
numb and weak even to kick. He was falling,

falling, and the darkness was rising to meet him. . .

Something gripped his heavy body, and he was thrust up through the water like a rocket through the sky. Air. He gulped and cried and gulped and cried.

'You're all right, son,' said Daddy. 'You're all right.'

Daddy was in the water beside him, holding him up and wedging him so that he couldn't go down again.

'You're all right.'

Slowly and gently Daddy moved himself and Jeremy James through the water and across to the bank. Jeremy James was coughing and spluttering like Daddy's car on a winter's day.

'I'll just lift you up on to the bank,' said Daddy, 'and then you must pull yourself to the top. All right?'

Daddy lifted him high on to the bank, and he gripped the grass tightly. Then he felt Daddy's hand on his bottom, pushing him upwards, and he crawled to the top and lay on his stomach.

He suddenly felt very cold, and his teeth began to chatter. He couldn't stop crying. Somehow the tears kept coming out like a bubbling fountain, joining the river water that flowed down from his hair, his ears and his mouth.

'Come on, Jeremy James,' said Daddy. 'I think that's enough fishing for today. Let's go home.' He lifted Jeremy James on to his shoulder. But the fishing hadn't quite finished. As Daddy picked up the fishing rod, there was an unmistakable pull on the line (which had fallen back into the water).

'Well I'm blowed,' said Daddy.

Jeremy James looked round to see what was blowing Daddy, and he saw a big silver fish flying slowly through the air towards him.

'Nice of him to wait for us, wasn't it?' said Daddy.

When Mummy heard what had happened, she shook her head from side to side like a fish shaking its tail.

'It was all my fault,' said Daddy. 'I was watching the fish instead of Jeremy James.'

Daddy and Jeremy James dripped upstairs, and took off all their wet clothes. Then Jeremy James sat down in the nicest hot bath anyone had ever had.

By the time they came downstairs, Jeremy James had stopped crying and shivering and tooth-chattering, and instead felt warm and fresh and clean. And when his nose took in a delicious smell coming from the kitchen, he suddenly realized that he was very, very hungry.

'What's for supper?' he asked Mummy.

'Guess,' said Mummy.

'Fish,' said Jeremy James.

'And whose fish?' asked Daddy.

'My fish,' said Jeremy James.

Of all the fish that Jeremy James had ever tasted, his fish proved to be the tastiest. Mummy and Daddy each had a piece as well, and they both said it was the best fish ever.

'Almost worth diving into the river for,' said Daddy.

All the same, Jeremy James decided he didn't want to go fishing again. Fishing, he thought, was very dangerous – and not just for maggots.

Do Goldfish Play the Violin?

The goldfish pond in Aunt Janet's garden must have been quite deep, because you couldn't see the bottom. What you could see was a sort of dark jungle down below, and lots of green leaves on the top with the goldfish swimming in between them. It was the goldfish that Jeremy James liked watching, though he kept well back from the edge of the pond to make sure he didn't fall in. He was also holding Jennifer's hand, and he certainly didn't want her to go fishing.

'Fish!' said Jennifer.

'Goldfish!' said Jeremy James.

'Go fish!' said Jennifer.

'No,' said Jeremy James. 'That's dangerous.'

The two families were in the garden. The grown-ups were sitting in deckchairs, and Melissa – who was the same age as Jeremy James – had just come out of the living room and was showing Christopher her new doll. Christopher was not interested in the new doll or in Melissa, and toddled hurriedly across the lawn to Mummy.

It was a happy, peaceful scene, with the sun shining, birds singing, bees buzzing, and everybody quietly and contentedly occupied. Then Aunt Janet made an announcement.

'Now, my dears, we're going to have a special treat. Is everything ready, Melissa?'

'Yes, Mummy,' said Melissa.

'Right, I want you all to come into the living room. The children, too. Come along, Jeremy James and Jennifer.'

They all trooped into the living room, where Aunt Janet asked everyone to sit down. Then Melissa put a sheet of paper on a strange-looking metal what's-a-name.

'Melissa,' said Aunt Janet, 'is going to play the violin for us.'

Melissa opened a black box and took out her violin.

'She's only been learning for six months,' said Aunt Janet, 'but she's *so* gifted. Are you ready, Melissa? Good. She's going to play six pieces by Sir Edward Elgar. Shush, everybody! Right, Melissa, dear, we're all listening.'

Melissa stood with her pigtails at the back of her neck and her violin at the front, and pulled a sort of stringy stick across the violin. The sound that came out went through the room like a needle through a buttonhole. The only similar sound Jeremy James had ever heard was

48

Christopher's raging screech when Jennifer snatched a toy from him. It was a high, piercing wail that shook your eardrums till your teeth rattled. Melissa's violin wail was not as loud as Christopher's, but it contained the same degree of pain.

Jeremy James stole a look at Mummy and Daddy. Mummy was sitting with a funny smile on her face, gazing straight at Melissa as if she were listening carefully. Daddy was also gazing at Melissa, but he had screwed up his eyes, which actually closed at one moment, and Jeremy James noticed that his mouth was shut tight, as if he were gritting his teeth.

Melissa stopped, and the grown-ups clapped while Aunt Janet cried, 'Well done, darling!'

The piece hadn't lasted long, and Jeremy James was about to get up when Aunt Janet spoke again:

'Now for the second piece.'

The second piece sounded exactly the same as the first, until Jeremy James thought there were two violins playing. The second violin, however, turned out to be Christopher whose wail contained some notes that Sir Edward Elgar had never imagined.

Mummy glanced apologetically at Aunt Janet, and slipped out into the garden with Christopher. Jeremy James managed not to glance at Aunt Janet, and he also slipped out into the garden. The scraping shrillness followed, but it didn't hurt quite so much from further away.

There was another light shower of applause from the living room, then Aunt Janet appeared at the patio door.

'Are you coming back in?' she asked.

'We'd better not,' said Mummy. 'Our Christopher's not a great music-lover, I'm afraid. But we can hear quite well anyway.'

Aunt Janet went back into the living room.

'I'm not a great music-lover either,' said Jeremy James.

From inside the living room they heard Daddy say, 'No, no, carry on. It's really. . . ugh, ugh. . . lovely.'

Mummy, Jeremy James and Christopher wandered down to look at the goldfish. They watched the fish dart through the leaves as swiftly as Melissa's bow darted over the wrong strings, and it was then that Jeremy James had an idea.

When Melissa had finished playing (and heavily defeating) Sir Edward Elgar, Mummy went to change the twin's nappies, Uncle Jack took Daddy out to see his new car, and Aunt Janet went to the kitchen to prepare tea. That left Jeremy James and Melissa to play games together. Jeremy James hated playing games with Melissa, but today was going to be different.

'Let's play Freezing,' he said.

He had played Freezing with Melissa once before. One person had to hide something, and the other tried to find it. The hider told the seeker he was freezing, cold, warm, or hot according to how near the seeker was. Melissa had found Jeremy James's sweet-wrapper in no time at all, but Jeremy James hadn't found his

toy car, which Melissa had hidden in her doll's knickers.

'Right,' said Melissa. 'I'll do the hiding.'

She hid a pin in the pocket of her dress, so that she could keep moving around making Jeremy James cold. But that was the trick she had used with the car and the doll, and it wasn't long before Jeremy James found the pin.

'Now I'll hide something,' said Jeremy James. 'Go in the front room till I call *ready*.'

'I'm only counting up to one hundred,' said Melissa, 'then I'm coming whether you're ready or not.'

Jeremy James had to be quick, and he *was* quick. By the time Melissa had reached one hundred, he was back in the living room and had closed the patio door.

Melissa searched the living room, and she searched Jeremy James, but she was freezing wherever she went.

'You'll never find it,' said Jeremy James. 'I've won.'

'No you haven't,' said Melissa. 'I know where it is.'

'Where?' said Jeremy James.

'It's in the garden,' said Melissa.

She opened the patio door.

'Just a bit warmer,' said Jeremy James.

Melissa went out into the garden, and the

further she went, the warmer she became.

'Very hot,' said Jeremy James at last. Melissa was standing on the edge of the goldfish pond.

'It's in the pond,' said Melissa.

'Right,' said Jeremy James.

'So I've won,' said Melissa.

'No you haven't,' said Jeremy James. 'Because you haven't found it yet.'

'Yes I have,' said Melissa. 'I've found it in the pond.'

'What is it, then?' asked Jeremy James.

'I don't know,' said Melissa.

'Then I've won,' said Jeremy James.

'No you haven't!' said Melissa.

'Yes I have,' said Jeremy James.

'It's not fair!' said Melissa.

'Yes it is,' said Jeremy James.

Melissa started crying, and Aunt Janet came out to see what was the matter, followed by Mummy a moment later. Melissa said Jeremy James had cheated, and Jeremy James said he hadn't, and Melissa's crying turned into a howling that reminded Jeremy James of Sir Headache Elgar.

Not even Uncle Jack or Daddy quite knew the rules of Freezing, and so no one could really say whether Jeremy James had cheated or not. The grown-ups therefore suggested the game should be called a draw, but Melissa said she'd won, and stamped off to her bedroom and slammed the door behind her.

'Oh dear!' said Aunt Janet, 'they do take these games so seriously, don't they?'

It was not until a couple of hours later, when Mummy, Daddy, the twins and Jeremy James were driving home, that an interesting question occurred to Daddy.

'Jeremy James,' he said, 'in that game of Freezing, what exactly *did* you throw in the goldfish pond?'

'The black box,' said Jeremy James.

'What black box?' asked Daddy.

'The black box with Melissa's violin,' said Jeremy James.

Daddy just managed to stop the car from swerving off the road, and Mummy let out a gasp that sounded just like one of Melissa's wrong notes.

As soon as they got home, Mummy telephoned Aunt Janet, while Daddy explained to Jeremy James that violins were very expensive, and throwing a violin into a goldfish pond could ruin it, as well as ruining the father who would have to pay for it.

'It was very naughty of you,' said Daddy, 'and you must never do such a thing again.'

'No, Daddy,' said Jeremy James.

'Though just between ourselves,' said Daddy, 'I'd sooner hear the goldfish play it than your cousin Melissa.'

Daddy wasn't a great music-lover either.

The Battleaxe

There was a very important lady coming to tea.

'Is it the Queen?' asked Jeremy James.

'Well, no,' said Daddy, 'she's not *that* important.'

'It's a lady who runs a theatre,' said Mummy, 'and that's very important for Daddy. So we must all be on our best behaviour. What's she like anyway, John?'

'A battleaxe,' said Daddy.

'What is a battleaxe?' asked Jeremy James.

'You'll see,' said Daddy.

'I hope she likes strawberries and cream,' said Mummy.

'*I* do,' said Jeremy James.

'I know you do,' said Mummy, 'but I've met you before, haven't I?'

Mummy prepared the things for tea, Daddy looked for things to show the lady, the twins played quietly – then loudly (Christopher hurt his finger) – in their playpen, and Jeremy James looked out of his bedroom window, watching for the very important lady. It was a pity she

wasn't as important as the Queen, but she was important enough for strawberries and cream, and if she was a sort of axe as well, she was worth watching for.

A big black car drew up outside the house, and Jeremy James rushed downstairs to Daddy's study.

'There's a big black car, Daddy!' he cried. 'It's the very important lady!'

The doorbell rang, and Daddy went into the hall, with Jeremy James right behind him.

'Hello, John,' said a deep voice.

'Hello, Lilian,' said Daddy. 'Lovely to see you. Come in.'

And in stepped. . . well, was it a man or a woman? Wide-eyed, Jeremy James peeped round Daddy at a pair of grey trousers, a grey jacket, a collar and tie, and a rather lined face under a bush of grey hair.

'Hello,' said the lady to Jeremy James.

Jeremy James's lips said, 'hello,' but his voice stayed behind and said nothing.

'This is Jeremy James,' said Daddy.

'Pleased to meet you, Jeremy James,' said the lady, and bent down to shake his hand. Jeremy James's arm flapped as limply as a broken wing, and his mouth gaped as if he were waiting to be fed.

Mummy came from the kitchen into the hall.

'This is my wife,' said Daddy. 'Darling, this is Lilian da Costa.'

There were more handshakes and pleased-to-meet-you's, and then the lady was introduced to the twins. Jennifer immediately pulled herself to her feet and smiled sweetly, but Christopher withdrew into the far corner of the playpen and looked very, very serious.

'Lovely children!' boomed the lady. 'You must be very proud of them.'

Christopher's serious face crumpled into tragedy.

'Wah!' he howled. 'Wah! Wah!'

'Oh dear,' said Mummy. 'He's a bit shy of strangers.'

Jeremy James was not surprised. There couldn't be many strangers that were stranger than this one.

Daddy took the lady into his study so that they could talk quietly, and when Mummy had calmed Christopher down, she and Jeremy James went into the kitchen together.

'Mummy,' said Jeremy James, 'is she a man?'

'Sh!' whispered Mummy, 'not so loud! No, she's a woman.'

'But she looks like a man!' whispered Jeremy James.

'I know,' said Mummy, 'but you don't get

men called Lilian. Now off you go to your room, and I'll call you when it's teatime.'

Jeremy James wandered upstairs. From Daddy's study came the sound of a deep voice that wasn't Daddy's. If a woman looked like a man and sounded like a man, why wasn't she a man? Perhaps, thought Jeremy James, that was what was meant by a battleaxe.

Jeremy James could hardly wait for tea, but not because of the strawberries. He wanted to see the important lady again. And he wanted to ask her some questions. So when Mummy at last called out, 'Jeremy James, it's time for . . .' he was already at the table in time for 'tea'.

Daddy and the lady were sitting there, and the lady was looking serious and saying: 'If the d. . . . . government keep slapping their d. . . . . taxes on theatre tickets, we shall all d. . . . . well be out of business!'

Jeremy James wondered if Mummy would tell the lady off for saying naughty words, but Mummy was pouring tea and didn't seem to have heard.

Jeremy James sat in his usual chair and looked at the lady.

Then the lady looked at Jeremy James.

'Now then, young man,' she said, 'what have you got to say for yourself?'

'Well,' said Jeremy James, 'are you *really* a woman?'

'Jeremy James!' exclaimed Mummy, pouring milk on to the table cloth.

'That's all right, my dear,' said the lady. 'Yes, Jeremy James, I am *really* a woman.'

'Then why have you got such a deep voice?' asked Jeremy James.

'Are you a man?' asked the lady.

'Well, nearly,' said Jeremy James.

'Then why have you got such a high voice?' asked the lady.

Jeremy James didn't know, but he thought his voice would get deeper when he grew older. Then the lady said that was exactly what had happened to *her* voice.

'And there's nothing,' said the lady, 'that you or I can do about it.'

'Well why do you wear men's clothes?' asked Jeremy James.

Daddy had a little fit of coughing, and Mummy waved her hands in the air and said Jeremy James had asked enough questions, but the lady smiled and said:

'I wear 'em because I like 'em. Would you like to wear a dress, Jeremy James?'

'No thank you,' said Jeremy James.

'Nor would I,' said the lady. 'So I don't. And nor do you.'

'Do have some more scones,' said Mummy, 'and Jeremy James, let's have less talk. Just get on with your tea.'

Mummy gave Jeremy James a buttered scone with jam on it, and at the same time asked the lady a question about her theatre. Jeremy James munched and listened wonderingly to the deep voice, while Mummy and Daddy nodded and occasionally murmured 'yes' or 'mhm' or 'of course'.

After the scones came the long-awaited strawberries and cream, so Jeremy James was far too busy to ask any questions. But when he'd finished (and the lady had only just *started* her strawberries), there was a sudden silence at the table, so that he was able to ask the question he'd been wanting to ask all afternoon.

'What *is* a battleaxe?'

The silence after this question was even more silent than the silence before. Eventually Mummy, whose face had gone a little white, said to no one in particular:

'I just don't know where he gets these words from!'

'From Daddy,' said Jeremy James.

'Ugh!' said Daddy.

Suddenly there was a most extraordinary noise. It was like elephant trumpet-calls with frog-croaks in between, and the calls and the croaks were all coming from the lady. She was laughing. And as she laughed, her shoulders shook and her head waggled up and down like a pecking bird. Jeremy James had never seen anyone laugh like that. It was a laugh that made you laugh just to hear it, and before long Jeremy James was laughing, Mummy and Daddy were laughing, and even Jennifer in the playpen was laughing. Only Christopher, on the other side of the playpen, had failed to notice anything funny.

It was a long time before the laughter died down, but at last the lady wiped her eyes, said, 'Oh dear!' several times, gave a couple more trumpet toots, and then shook her head from side to side.

'So you want to know. . . toot. . . what a battleaxe is,' she said. 'Well, Jeremy James, a battleaxe is a strong and bossy woman who gets what she wants because she's strong and bossy. I am a battleaxe.'

'No, really. . .' said Daddy.

'Do you always get what you want?' asked Jeremy James.

'Always,' said the lady. 'Shall I prove it?'

'Yes,' said Jeremy James.

'Right,' said the lady. 'I want you to have some more strawberries.'

Jeremy James looked at the lady, and the lady looked at Jeremy James, and they both started smiling again. Then Jeremy James looked at Mummy, Mummy looked at the lady, the lady looked at Mummy, and Mummy looked at Jeremy James. Mummy put some more strawberries in Jeremy James's bowl.

'Now I want you to eat 'em,' said the lady.

Thus the lady proved that she always got

what she wanted. And when Mummy asked her if *she* would like some more strawberries, she also proved that she got what she liked.

The rest of tea was very jolly and everyone laughed a lot, especially when the lady laughed. Jeremy James was really sorry when at last she said it was time for her to leave.

'I want you to stay,' he said.

'If you were a battleaxe,' said the lady, 'I'd have to, but you're not, and I can't.'

She kissed Mummy and Daddy goodbye, and asked if she could have a kiss from Jeremy James. He gave her a very big warm smacky one.

'I haven't laughed so much in years,' she said to Daddy. 'You ought to put your family on the stage to cheer everyone up.'

Jeremy James waved until the big black car had disappeared, and then asked Mummy what had made the lady laugh so much. Mummy explained that Daddy's calling her a battleaxe had been a sort of secret, because 'battleaxe' was a rather rude word.

'Some people would have been angry,' said Mummy, 'but Mrs da Costa thought it was funny. Fortunately.'

Jeremy James didn't see why anyone should be angry.

'I think,' said Jeremy James, 'that battleaxes are nice. And I wish I was one.'

How to Stop Paying Bills

It was Jeremy James's job to fetch the post in the morning. Most of it was for Daddy, and came in printed brown envelopes which made Daddy say, 'Ugh!' Mummy's letters were usually hand-written, and Jeremy James only had post at Christmas time and on his birthday. He would have liked more letters, and he would also have liked more Christmases and more birthdays.

On this particular morning, there had only been one letter – a printed brown envelope for Daddy.

'Ugh!' said Daddy. 'Another bill.'

He opened the brown envelope, took out a printed piece of paper, unfolded it, and said, 'Oh!'

'How much?' asked Mummy.

'Seventy-two pounds,' said Daddy.

Then Mummy said, 'Oh!' as well.

'What exactly *are* bills?' asked Jeremy James.

'A worple worple nuisance,' said Daddy.

'Bills,' said Mummy, 'are what you pay for

66

things like gas, water, electricity, the phone. Whatever you use has to be paid for, and you know how much to pay when you get the bill.'

For the rest of the day, when he wasn't playing, eating, going for a walk with Mummy and the twins, or thinking about other things, Jeremy James thought about bills. If Daddy didn't have bills, he would be richer. And if Daddy were richer, Jeremy James might get more pocket money. But how could Jeremy James save Daddy from paying bills?

It was when Jeremy James was helping Mummy in the garden that the seed of an idea sowed itself in his mind. They were pulling up weeds, which they were throwing into a rubbish bag.

'Weeds,' said Mummy, 'are a nuisance.'

'Are they a worple worple nuisance?' asked Jeremy James.

'Yes,' said Mummy.

'Then they're just like bills,' said Jeremy James.

That night, before he went to sleep, Jeremy James thought long and hard about Daddy and bills and rubbish bags. He remembered that only yesterday Daddy had bitten into an apple which had had a maggot in it, and Daddy had thrown it in the rubbish. ('Thank heaven,' said Daddy, 'it wasn't *half* a maggot.') If bad things

were thrown away, why didn't Daddy throw his bills away?

The next morning, when Jeremy James went downstairs, Daddy was in the kitchen searching for something.

'You haven't seen the sugar, have you, Jeremy James?' asked Daddy.

'I saw Mummy pour sugar into that blue tin,' said Jeremy James.

'Ah yes,' said Daddy, 'the sugar tin. I didn't think of that.'

Of course! Daddy would never think of looking for sugar in the sugar tin, or for shoes in the shoe cupboard or clothes in the clothes cupboard. So why should he think of throwing bills in the rubbish bag?

Jeremy James thought of telling Daddy about his bright idea, but grown-ups sometimes didn't understand bright ideas. They certainly hadn't understood his clever way of beating Melissa at 'Freezing'. And they hadn't understood why he'd once stopped a train, and once fed an elephant, and once taken a tin of mandarin oranges from the bottom of the pile. No, he had better keep his bright idea to himself and see what he could do without the grown-ups.

That morning there were two letters. One was hand-written, and Jeremy James gave it to Mummy. The other was printed and brown, and Jeremy James took it up to his bedroom and buried it under a pile of cars and planes and books and trains.

'Nothing for me?' asked Daddy.

'Nothing,' said Jeremy James.

Daddy didn't seem pleased that there was nothing for him, but on the other hand he didn't say, 'Ugh!'

As the days stretched into weeks, so the pile of hidden letters grew bigger and bigger. Jeremy James wondered how much money he'd already saved Daddy, and he also wondered when a richer Daddy would make a richer Jeremy James.

'Daddy,' he asked one day, 'if you had more money, would you give me more pocket money?'

'I expect so,' said Daddy.

'Well,' said Jeremy James, 'I was just wondering if perhaps you did have more money.'

'More money than what?' asked Daddy.

'More money than before,' said Jeremy James.

'More money than before what?' asked Daddy.

Jeremy James thought for a moment. 'Well, more money than before now,' he said.

Daddy turned to Mummy who had just

come in with a heavy shopping basket.

'Our eldest child,' he said, 'is asking for a rise.'

'I don't blame him,' said Mummy, 'with the price things are today. I'd ask for one myself if we could afford it.'

Jeremy James suggested that they *could* afford it now that they weren't paying any bills, but Daddy simply looked surprised and asked why Jeremy James thought they weren't paying any bills.

'Because,' said Jeremy James, 'I haven't brought you any.'

'Yes, it has been rather a quiet period,' said Daddy. 'They'll probably all come together. Just before Christmas.'

But they didn't all come together. They came one at a time, and one at a time they found their way upstairs to their secret hiding-place. Unfortunately Daddy, who had never realized that bills could be thrown away, still didn't realize that he now had no bills to pay. Nor did he realize that he was richer than he had been before. And so he didn't realize that he could give Jeremy James *and* Mummy a rise. That was the trouble with a Daddy who didn't think of things.

There was a different kind of trouble ahead, though, and it was trouble that made Daddy,

Mummy and Jeremy James do quite a lot of thinking. Daddy had gone into town with Jeremy James, leaving Mummy at home with Christopher and Jennifer, and when they had come back they had found Mummy looking even grumblier than Daddy had looked in the days when he used to receive bills.

'What's the matter?' asked Daddy.

'It's the telephone man,' said Mummy. 'They've cut our phone off.'

'Cut our phone off?' cried Daddy.

'They say we haven't paid our bill!' said Mummy.

'Haven't paid our bill?' cried Daddy.

'I told them there must be some mistake,' said Mummy, 'but they said we'd had a bill and a reminder and a final warning!'

'Final warning?' cried Daddy.

'And now they've cut it off,' said Mummy.

Jeremy James didn't quite know what was meant by cutting a phone off, but it sounded very painful indeed.

'We haven't even had a bill, let alone a final warning!' cried Daddy. 'I shall ring them up straight away.'

'You can't,' said Mummy. 'You've nothing to ring them with.'

Jeremy James had a sort of burning feeling behind his eyes, and his heart seemed to have

slipped down into his tummy. Perhaps it was time to tell Mummy and Daddy about his bright idea, which might not have been so bright after all.

'Mummy,' he said.

'Yes, dear?' asked Mummy.

'Um. . . if we found the bill, would they stick the phone back on again?'

'If we found it and paid it they would,' said Mummy.

Jeremy James ran upstairs to his room, flung books and planes and cars and trains in all directions, and came downstairs again with an armful of printed brown envelopes.

Daddy's mouth opened and shut as if an elephant had just sat on his car, and Mummy's eyes went as wide and round as a telephone dial.

'Where on earth did these come from?' Mummy asked.

Jeremy James told them all about his bright idea which might not have been so bright. When he had finished, there was a long silence. At last Daddy reached down, took all the brown envelopes, and said:

'I've told you before about these bright ideas, Jeremy James. In future, would you please speak before you act.'

'The trouble is,' said Mummy, 'if you don't pay your bills, you can't have any more light or heat or phone or even your house. They'll all get taken away, Jeremy James.'

'I didn't know that,' said Jeremy James.

'You didn't think,' said Daddy. 'I suppose you meant well, but you just didn't think. Now I suppose I'd better go and write out some cheques.'

With a grumbly face he went into his study and closed the door behind him.

'Next time you get a bright idea, Jeremy James,' said Mummy, 'you'll tell us, won't you?'

'Yes, Mummy,' said Jeremy James.

Daddy opened his study door.

'You haven't seen my cheque book, have you?' he asked.

'Probably in your jacket,' said Mummy. 'In a leather case marked *cheque book*.'

'Ah,' said Daddy. 'Thanks. I didn't think of that.'

The Magician

'Now watch carefully!' said The Great Marvello.

Jeremy James watched carefully.

'You see this empty cone?'

Jeremy James saw the empty cone.

'You see this black cloth?'

Jeremy James saw the black cloth.

'I place this black cloth. . . nothing in it, you see, just a plain black cloth. . . over the empty cone. . . so. I pick up the cone. . . so. . . I pass the cloth through the cone . . . and out . . . comes . . .'

And out came one, two, three white doves, which fluttered into the air and came to rest on the magician's outstretched arm.

Jeremy James gasped, and Mummy and Daddy applauded.

'How did he do it, Mummy?' asked Jeremy James.

'No idea,' said Mummy.

'How did he do it, Daddy?' asked Jeremy James.

'Couldn't tell you,' said Daddy.

'Where did the birds come from?' asked Jeremy James, hoping that someone in the hall would tell him. But nobody else could hear him, apart from Mummy and Daddy, because the applause was so loud. So Jeremy James waited till the applause had ended. Then he asked again, 'Where did the birds come from?'

A few people laughed, and some heads turned round, and Mummy whispered, 'We don't know, Jeremy James. Let's watch the next trick.'

But The Great Marvello had heard the question, and a little smile glinted from behind the black beard. In his shining black suit and red cape he stepped down from the stage, like a god from a mountain, and walked slowly up the aisle.

'For my next trick,' he announced as he walked, 'I shall need a little help from the audience.'

Jeremy James's eyes became rounder and rounder as the great man approached, and he held his breath with excitement, willing The Great Marvello to come to him.

'I need a man,' said the magician.

Jeremy James wanted to shout out, 'Daddy's a man!' but he couldn't move or speak in the ever nearer presence of the magic man.

'A man and wife,' said the magician. 'Or perhaps a man and child.'

'Me!' cried Jeremy James's voice before he could even think of stopping it.

'Aha!' said the great man, drawing level with Jeremy James.

'Oh Lord!' said Daddy.

'You'd like to help?' Marvello asked Jeremy James.

'Yes, please!' said Jeremy James.

'Would you mind, sir?' Marvello asked Daddy.

'Ugh ugh,' said Daddy, 'um. . . well I'd. . .'

'Splendid!' said Marvello. 'A couple of good sports. Come with me then, please.'

A hall full of smiling faces watched as Jeremy James marched up on stage behind Marvello, while Daddy, red-faced, followed several paces behind. They told the magician their names, and then Marvello asked Daddy for his wrist watch.

'Now then, Jeremy James,' said Marvello, 'I want you to look into this paper bag and tell me what you see.'

Jeremy James looked into the paper bag and announced that he could see nothing. Daddy could see nothing either.

'Right,' said Marvello. 'And now I shall put the watch into the paper bag.'

In it went, and he closed the bag, folded over the top, and handed it to Jeremy James.

'Can you still feel the watch in there, Jeremy James?' he asked.

Jeremy James could.

'Now I want you to put the bag under this black cloth,' said the magician.

Jeremy James put the bag with Daddy's watch under the black cloth. Then the magician showed them both another empty bag which Jeremy James had to put under another black cloth on the other side of the table. And so there were now two bags under two cloths, one at either end of the table. Then from somewhere that Jeremy James didn't see, Marvello produced a very large hammer.

'Oh no!' said Daddy.

'Oh yes!' said Marvello. 'I want you to take this hammer, John, and smash your watch.'

Daddy didn't want to do it, but the magician and Jeremy James both said he should, and so he did. Then Marvello allowed Jeremy James to hammer the watch too, 'just to make sure.' After that he invited Daddy to lift up the black cloth and open the paper bag with his smashed watch in it. This Daddy did, only to find that his watch wasn't there.

'Now, Jeremy James,' said the magician, 'I

want you to lift the other cloth and open the other paper bag.'

Inside the other paper bag, what did Jeremy James find? He found Daddy's unsmashed watch.

Everyone in the hall clapped very loudly, and the magician asked them to give Daddy and Jeremy James a special clap as they went back to their seats.

Jeremy James had never seen anything so wonderful as the trick with Daddy's watch. He talked about it all the way home, and at home he told the baby-sitter all about it, and next morning he told Christopher and Jennifer all about it, and next afternoon he told Richard and Trevor all about it. And the day after next, when he met Timothy from next door, he told him all about it too.

'I've seen that trick a dozen times,' said Timothy. 'It's easy.'

'It isn't,' said Jeremy James. 'It's magic.'

'Magic poo,' said Timothy. 'Anyone can do that trick.'

'I'll bet you can't,' said Jeremy James.

'Oh yes I can,' said Timothy.

'All right,' said Jeremy James, 'show me, then.'

Together they went to Timothy's house.

'Hello, Jeremy,' said Mrs Smyth-Fortescue

(who never called him Jeremy James). 'Have you come to play with Timothy?'

'Hello, Mrs Smite-Fortytwo,' said Jeremy James, 'Timothy wants to show me a trick.'

'Oh, that's nice,' said Mrs Smyth-Fortescue.

'I want two paper bags,' said Timothy, 'and two bits of cloth.'

'Please,' said Mrs Smyth-Fortescue.

'Now,' said Timothy.

Mrs Smyth-Fortescue provided the paper bags and two tea-towels. Then Timothy himself went to fetch his father's big hammer.

'Oh dear,' said Mrs Smyth-Fortescue, 'that looks a little dangerous.'

'No it isn't,' said Timothy. 'I'm only going to hit a paper bag.'

Timothy led the way upstairs to his room, and there he took off his brand new wrist watch, which his Daddy had just brought back from America. Then he opened the first paper bag and put the watch inside.

'Now put it under the cloth,' said Timothy.

Jeremy James put it under the tea-towel at one end of Timothy's table.

'Now look in the other bag,' said Timothy.

Jeremy James looked in the other bag.

'What's in it?' asked Timothy.

'Nothing,' said Jeremy James.

'Put it under the other cloth,' said Timothy.

Jeremy James put it under the other tea-towel at the other end of Timothy's table.

'Right!' said Timothy. 'Now watch!'

He picked up the hammer and raised it high in the air.

'Are you sure. . .?' Jeremy James started to ask, as Timothy brought the hammer down with a tremendous crash on to the first paper bag.

'You can hit it, too, if you like,' said Timothy generously.

But Jeremy James didn't want to.

'Coward!' said Timothy. 'There's nothing to be scared of.'

Jeremy James wasn't scared. He just had a funny feeling that Timothy shouldn't be doing this trick.

'All right,' said Timothy. 'Have a look in the bag.'

Jeremy James took off the first tea-towel, picked up the first bag, and looked inside. What did he find? He found Timothy's smashed watch.

He showed it to Timothy, whose face went almost as white as Marvello's doves. Timothy grabbed the second bag and opened it. What did he find? He found nothing.

'I've smashed my watch!' said Timothy.

'Yes,' said Jeremy James.

'What was that terrible crash?' asked Mrs Smyth-Fortescue, poking her head round Timothy's door.

'It was Timothy's trick,' said Jeremy James. 'But it didn't work.'

When Jeremy James told Mummy and Daddy about Timothy's trick, they both shook their heads and said, 'Ts! Ts!' and, 'What a silly boy!'

'I expect it was an expensive watch, too,' said Mummy.

'I know why the trick didn't work,' said Jeremy James.

'Why?' asked Daddy.

'Because,' said Jeremy James, 'it was the wrong watch. He should have used Daddy's.'

The Robbers

'Ugh!' said Daddy. 'Oh dear, oh dear! Hmmph! Ugh!'

Jeremy James had just brought Daddy a long white printed envelope which the postman had popped through the letter box.

'What is it, John?' asked Mummy.

'It's. . . ugh, hmmph. . . from the bank manager,' said Daddy.

'Oh dear,' said Mummy.

'He wants me to go and see him,' said Daddy.

'Oh dear, oh dear,' said Mummy.

'It appears,' said Daddy, 'that we are overdrawn.'

'Oh dear, oh dear, oh dear,' said Mummy.

Jeremy James didn't know what 'overdrawn' meant, but it didn't seem a very good thing to be, and when he asked Daddy who had 'overdrawed' him, Daddy pulled a long face and said that he had overdrawn himself.

'It means,' said Mummy, as Daddy *hmmphed* and *ughed* through the letter for the fourth time, 'that we've taken more out of the bank then we've put in. So now we owe the bank some money.'

'I've got 20p in my money box,' said Jeremy James. 'Though I was going to buy some liquorice-all-sorts with that.'

'Thanks,' said Daddy, 'but the bank manager wants more than liquorice-all-sorts, I'm afraid.'

It was decided that Mummy should go shopping with the twins, while Daddy and Jeremy James went to the bank. Then they would meet afterwards and come home together.

'What do banks do?' asked Jeremy James on the way.

'They look after your money,' said Daddy. 'If you have any.'

'Why?' asked Jeremy James.

'So that people can't steal it from you,' said Daddy.

'Can't they steal it from banks?' asked Jeremy James.

Daddy said they could, but it was difficult. Jeremy James wondered if he should ask the bank to look after his 20p, but Daddy reckoned that was too little. Jeremy James said it was more than Daddy had, and if the bank was looking after Daddy's less-than-nothing, it could also look after 20p. Daddy said,

'Hmmph!' and 'Ugh!' and by now they'd reached the bank.

Inside the bank was a queue of people at a long counter, and Jeremy James saw a girl behind the counter giving a thick wad of notes to a bald man in a suit. The man said, 'Thank you,' put the money in his wallet, and walked off.

'Daddy!' cried Jeremy James. 'That lady's giving money away! Why don't we get some from her?'

'I wish we could,' said Daddy, 'but it's like your money box – what doesn't go in can't come out.'

Daddy went up to a young lady at the very end of the counter and asked her something.

'I'll see if he's free,' said the young lady, and Daddy and Jeremy James sat down on two chairs in the corner.

'How do you steal from a bank?' asked Jeremy James.

'The usual way,' said Daddy, 'is to get a gun and say "stick 'em up". But I wouldn't try it if I were you.'

The young lady opened a door in the end wall.

'Mr Stoneheart will see you now,' she said.

'Right,' said Daddy. 'You wait here, Jeremy James. I shan't be long.'

Daddy straightened his tie, gave a little cough, took a deep breath, and passed through the door in the end wall.

Jeremy James sat watching the queue of people at the long counter. Some gave money in, and some took money out, and there seemed to be a lot more taker-outers than giver-inners. It might not be a bad idea, thought Jeremy James, to go and join the queue, just to see if he could be one of the taker-outers. That would give Daddy a nice surprise.

Jeremy James was about to jump down from his chair when he suddenly saw something that made him pause. The something that he saw was two young men who had just joined the queue. Jeremy James would have had to stand behind them, and he decided at once that he didn't want to stand anywhere near them. One had a lot of black bristle on his face, while the other had a scarf over his mouth and chin, and they both wore dirty raincoats and looked very rough.

Slowly they moved towards the head of the queue. The bristly man put a cigarette in his mouth and gave one to the scarfy man. Then the bristly man reached into his raincoat pocket and brought out. . . Jeremy James's eyes went as round as 10p pieces. The bristly man was holding a gun.

If you want to steal from a bank, Daddy had said, get a gun. But if you don't want them to steal from a bank, thought Jeremy James, get Daddy.

He walked boldly to the door in the end wall, turned the handle, and went in.

A grey-haired man with a grey moustache and a grey suit was sitting opposite the door behind a desk, and Daddy was sitting with his back to the door, saying, 'Er . . . worple . . . um . . . ugh . . .'

'Hello,' said the grey-haired man, 'what's this?'

Daddy turned round.

'Oh!' he said. 'Um. . . this is my son. What is it, Jeremy James?'

'There are two men with guns in the bank,' said Jeremy James.

'*Two men with guns?*' echoed the grey-haired man.

'Now hold on, Jeremy James,' said Daddy, 'are you sure. . .'

'*Are you sure?*' echoed the grey-haired man.

'Oh yes,' said Jeremy James, 'they've come to steal from the bank.'

The grey-haired man pressed a button on his desk, leapt out of his chair, banged his knee on a sharp corner, said a word Mummy had

absolutely forbidden, limped to a door in the far
wall and hurried out.

'Are you sure they had guns?' asked Daddy.

'Well, one of them did,' said Jeremy James.
'And the other one had a scarf.'

'He'll have a job holding up the bank with a
scarf,' said Daddy.

Suddenly bells started ringing, and from inside the bank Daddy and Jeremy James heard someone shouting. Jeremy James wanted to open the door so they could see what was happening, but Daddy said they must stay where they were in case the gunmen started shooting, or the scarfman started scarfing.

Then the bells stopped ringing, and everything was very quiet.

'Everything's very quiet,' said Daddy.

'Can we have a look?' asked Jeremy James.

'No,' said Daddy. 'It may be a gun with a silencer.'

They waited and waited, until at last the bank manager came back with a policeman, who looked very tall and very serious.

'This,' said the bank manager, 'is the young man who gave the alarm. And this is the young man's father.'

'Morning, sir,' said the policeman.

'Um. . . good morning, Officer,' said Daddy.

'What's your name, son?' asked the policeman.

'Jeremy James,' said Jeremy James.

'Well, Jeremy James,' said the policeman, 'the two men you saw were not here to rob the bank.'

'Oh dear,' said Daddy.

'And what you thought was a gun,' said the policeman, 'was a cigarette lighter.'

'Oh dear, oh dear,' said Daddy, 'I'm extremely sorry, but. . .'

'However,' said the policeman.

'However?' said Daddy.

'Although they weren't here to rob the bank,' said the policeman, 'they happen to be two villains that we've been after for quite some time. And as a matter of fact, there is a substantial reward for information leading to their capture.'

'A reward?' echoed Daddy.

'A substantial reward,' said the policeman. 'You've got a smart lad there, sir. You can be proud of him.'

'I certainly am,' said Daddy.

Then they all went out into the bank itself, and people crowded round Jeremy James and said what a smart lad he was. Jeremy James had a feeling that he wasn't so smart, since the bank robbers hadn't really been bank robbers at all, but he didn't tell anyone he wasn't so smart, because he wasn't so stupid.

'Now about that overdraft of yours,' said the bank manager when all the fuss had ended and the policeman had gone and the people had moved away. 'I'm sure you'll put it right in no time.'

'Yes, of course,' said Daddy.

'So let's forget about it, shall we?' said the bank manager.

'I'll be pleased to,' said Daddy.

The bank manager accompanied them all the way to the door of the bank, shook them both by the hand, and told them – with his last words of farewell – that the bank would always be at their service.

Daddy and Jeremy James met Mummy and the twins as planned, but they didn't go straight home. They stopped at the coffee-shop, and Jeremy James was allowed to choose any piece of cake he liked. Then, while he sat and ate his chocolate gateau and drank his Coca Cola, Daddy told Mummy the whole story.

'Well done, Jeremy James,' said Mummy.

'So what do you think of banks?' asked Daddy.

Jeremy James thought for a moment. After all, if it *had* been a gun and if he hadn't been there, the two men could easily have taken all the money out of the bank.

'Banks are all right,' he said, 'but I think I'll keep my 20p at home.'

Mr Blooming

It was snowing. The world through the window was a moving blur of dots and flickers, just like the television set when Daddy was trying to adjust it. Slowly everything was turning white, and yet even when the snowflakes brushed against the glass, they made no noise. They were silent and magical, like a ghost painting.

'What *is* snow?' asked Jeremy James.

'A blooming nuisance,' said Daddy.

'It's a sort of rain that freezes and falls from the sky,' said Mummy.

'It looks nice,' said Jeremy James.

'So does the river,' said Daddy. 'Until you fall in it.'

'You can go out and play in it if you like,' said Mummy.

'No thank you,' said Daddy.

'Yes please,' said Jeremy James.

And so Jeremy James was wrapped up in a coat, scarf and gloves, with wellington boots down below and woollen hat on top. Then he stepped out on to the ankle-deep carpet that was the back garden.

The snow was still falling, and one or two flakes touched his face. They were as cool as ice cream, and he wondered what flavour they were. He opened his mouth and tilted his head back till a snowflake fell in. There was no flavour at all. Just a quick, cold tingle.

'I wish they made strawberry-flavour snow,' said Jeremy James.

He scrunched through the garden leaving giant footprints behind him, and then he scrunched back to make the footprints even more giant. After that he threw handfuls of snow at nothing in particular, and found that most of it either blew back into his face or trickled down his wrists and into his sleeves or gloves. It was very wet.

'Having fun?' asked Daddy's voice.

Jeremy James hadn't even heard Daddy coming, but there he stood, as muffled up as Jeremy James and eyes shining just as brightly.

'How would you like to build a snowman?' he asked.

'Yes, please,' said Jeremy James.

'Great!' said Daddy. 'I haven't built a snowman since I was a boy.'

Jeremy James laughed.

'You weren't a boy, were you, Daddy?'

'Of course I was,' said Daddy.

'Funny,' said Jeremy James. 'I don't remember that.'

Jeremy James and Daddy set to work building a pile of snow. Daddy packed it all tightly together so that it was really hard, and Jeremy James kept bringing handfuls to pat into the pile Daddy had made.

Gradually it grew taller and taller, and eventually Daddy stood back and said:

'Right, that's the body. Now for the head.'

'Where are his legs?' asked Jeremy James.

'Ah!' said Daddy. 'Well he's wearing a long white coat.'

Jeremy James looked hard at the pile, and it *did* look a bit like a long white coat. But even a man in a long white coat would have arms.

'Ah!' said Daddy. 'Well his arms are behind his back.'

Jeremy James looked hard at the pile, and it *did* look a bit like a man with arms behind his back.

'Let's do his head,' said Daddy.

Together they rolled up a big ball, lifted it, and stuck it on top of the pile.

'There we are,' said Daddy. 'That's the head.'

'Where are his eyes and nose and mouth?' asked Jeremy James.

'You'll make a good critic,' said Daddy. 'But you're right – he *has* got a rather blank expression.'

Two pebbles, a clothes peg and an old clay pipe soon changed that, and Jeremy James found himself looking at a bald-headed man in a long white coat with his arms behind his back.

'How does he look?' asked Daddy.

'He looks cold,' said Jeremy James.

'Right again,' said Daddy, and put his hat on the snowman's head and his scarf round the snowman's neck.

'Now *you* look cold,' said Jeremy James.

'What are we going to call him?' asked Daddy.

Jeremy James thought for a moment.

'Mr Blooming,' he said.

'Why Mr Blooming?' asked Daddy.

'Because he's made of blooming snow,' said Jeremy James.

Jeremy James was very proud of Mr Blooming (and so was Daddy), and he looked out at him from the living room window several times during the day, just to make sure he was still there. And he *was* still there, calmly smoking his pipe and looking up at the house with his arms behind his back.

'Can we give him something to eat?' Jeremy James asked Mummy.

'I don't think he'd like our food,' said Mummy.

'I'll bet he likes strawberry ice cream,' said Jeremy James.

But Mummy thought it was too cold for ice cream.

'Then can we give him some soup?' asked Jeremy James.

'Soup isn't good for snowmen,' said Mummy.

'It's only good for Soupermen,' said Daddy.

'Well what *can* we give him?' asked Jeremy James.

But Mummy and Daddy said there was nothing they could give him, because snowmen didn't eat and didn't drink anything except snow.

Just before he went to bed, Jeremy James crept into the twins' room and looked out of their window (his own bedroom was at the front of the house). It had stopped snowing. Mr Blooming was standing in the middle of the white lawn, and Jeremy James waved to him.

'I hope you won't get hungry in the night,' he whispered.

Next morning, Jeremy James woke up and

looked out of his window. Most of the snow had gone. He rushed into the twins' room.

'Jem Jem!' cried Jennifer, pulling herself to her feet.

But Jeremy James didn't have time to talk to Jennifer. He ran straight to the window. Mr Blooming was still there – but somehow he looked different. There was some green grass around him now, but it wasn't the green that

had changed him. No, he was smaller – his head had sunk, and the hat had fallen over his face.

'I knew he'd get hungry!' cried Jeremy James, and ran downstairs.

Mummy was in the kitchen.

'Good morning, Jeremy James,' she said. 'You're bright and early. What's the matter?'

'It's Mr Blooming!' said Jeremy James. 'He's hungry.'

Mummy looked out of the window.

'I'm afraid he's melting,' she said.

'No, he needs some snow,' said Jeremy James. 'He wants his breakfast!'

Mummy helped Jeremy James get dressed quickly, and out he raced into the garden.

'I'm coming, Mr Blooming!' he cried, and stooped to pick up a handful of snow. But the snow was not like yesterday's – it was soft and mushy, and dripped through Jeremy James's fingers. He carried what was left of it to Mr Blooming, and pressed it against his mouth, but all that happened was that the pipe fell out, and the breakfast snow simply dripped on to Mr Blooming's scarf.

Jeremy James could see now that Mr Blooming's body had shrunk to only half the size it had been.

'It's no good, I'm afraid,' said Mummy's

voice behind him. 'Once snow starts to melt, there's nothing you can do.'

Gently she tipped Mr Blooming's hat back so that it wasn't over his eyes.

'Snow is only water, you see,' she said.

'Maybe he'd eat some strawberry ice cream,' said Jeremy James. 'Ice cream is like snow, Mummy, isn't it?'

'I'll tell you what,' said Mummy. 'You can give him a spoonful of ice cream, and if he eats it, you can give him some more.'

She went back into the kitchen, and brought out the tub of ice cream and a spoon. But when Jeremy James tried to put the spoon into Mr Blooming's mouth, the ice cream fell off and plopped on to the ground below.

'He won't eat it,' said Jeremy James.

'No,' said Mummy. 'Snowmen only eat snow.'

Sadly Jeremy James went back into the house with Mummy. But all through breakfast he gazed out of the window at Mr Blooming. It didn't make him feel any better either when Daddy came into the room.

'Not a bad morning. At least the blooming snow has gone.'

Mummy pointed silently towards Jeremy James and then towards the garden. Daddy put his hand to his mouth and murmured, 'Sorry!'

Then Mummy went upstairs to see to the twins, and Daddy sat down beside Jeremy James.

'I've been thinking,' he said. 'Next time it snows, we'll build a proper snowman. We'll buy a mask to use as a face, and we'll give him a jacket so that he's got arms. What do you think, Jeremy James?'

'Mr Blooming *is* a proper snowman,' said Jeremy James.

'Well, yes, he is,' said Daddy. 'But the next one will be even more proper.'

'When's it going to snow again?' asked Jeremy James.

'I don't know,' said Daddy. 'But if you get yourself ready, we'll go and buy that mask now, in case it snows tomorrow.'

By the time Jeremy James and Daddy came back from town with their mask and with a bag of shopping for Mummy, there was very little of Mr Blooming left: just a tiny ball of snow, a hat and a scarf, two pebbles, a peg and a pipe. Jeremy James and Daddy stood looking sadly down.

'Daddy,' said Jeremy James, 'will I melt like that one day?'

Daddy thought for a moment.

'Do you drink soup?' he asked.

'Yes,' said Jeremy James.

'And do you eat ice cream?'.

'Yes,' said Jeremy James.

'Then you won't melt,' said Daddy. 'At least not for a very long time.'

Cold Nativity

'I thick I cad see a star,' said Jeremy James.

'Oh dear,' creaked the voice of the Reverend Cole as the Reverend Cole creaked towards the platform. 'Can't you say 'think' and. . . um. . . 'can'?'

'Do,' said Jeremy James. 'I've got a code.'

'Oh dear,' said the Reverend Cole again, 'a shepherd with a cold. Well, do . . . um . . . the best you can.'

'I thick I cad see a star,' said Jeremy James, 'shidig over Bethleheb.'

'Over where?' cried the Reverend Cole.

'Bethleheb,' said Jeremy James.

It was the dress rehearsal of the Sunday School Nativity Play, and Jeremy James wasn't enjoying it very much. Nor was the Reverend Cole. His shepherd was not the only one with a cold – Joseph had one as well. And his was so bad that he hadn't even come to the rehearsal. A Nativity Play without Joseph is rather like stuffing without turkey. The Virgin Mary was there all right, and so was the baby Jesus, which being a china doll had managed to avoid catching a cold. But there were only two wise men, and one of those was little Trevor who, for a wise man, had a terrible memory and could never remember any of his six lines.

Jeremy James had a very good memory. His memory was so good that he knew almost every line of the whole play. But no matter what line he spoke today, it was full of sniffs and d's and b's.

Fat Richard, who was the inn-keeper, also had a cold, and when he informed Mary that

there was 'no roob at the idd', the Reverend Cole sat down in a pew, put his head in his hands, and groaned.

'We can't go on!' he cried.

The Reverend Cole was very old, and very tired. He had produced a Nativity Play every Christmas for the last thirty-five years, but now he vowed that the thirty-sixth would be his last. There had, of course, been disasters in the past. Once he had lost Joseph to a flu epidemic and had actually taken the part himself (which he enjoyed, because he liked acting) – but there had never been a rehearsal quite as disastrous as this one. The Nativity, he reckoned, would be the death of him.

'It's no good!' he cried. 'Everybody go home, wrap up warm, take vitamin C, and pray for a miracle. I want you back here at nine o'clock in the morning for a final run-through.'

Mummy was waiting for Jeremy James at the back of the church.

'How did it go?' she asked.

'Dot very well,' said Jeremy James. 'Bister Cole wasert very pleased, add we have to go back toborrow at dide o'clock.'

By nine o'clock the following morning, some of the Reverend Cole's prayers had been answered. There had indeed been one or two miracles. For one thing, his Joseph was there and ready to do his part. For another, the third wise man was there as well. And the Lord had also been merciful to Richard and to Jeremy James, because both of them were now able to say 'Bethlehem' and 'inn'.

With such blessings, one might have thought that the Reverend Cole's problems were over. However, Joseph's return had been balanced by the Virgin Mary's absence. Sarah Goody had been struck down by illness, and under no circumstances would her parents allow her to leave her bed since she had been so sick in the night.

The recovery of the other actors had to be paid for by the Reverend Cole himself. By nine o'clock his aged eyes were streaming, his old nose was blocked, and he was cursing himself for not having retired last year.

If a Nativity Play without Joseph is like stuffing without turkey, a Nativity Play without the Virgin Mary is like Christmas dinner without turkey, stuffing, *and* Christmas pudding. The situation was hopeless. Not even the Reverend Cole could possibly pass for the Virgin Mary.

'It's do good,' he said to the children. 'We cart go od without a Virgid Bary.'

'I could be the Virgin Mary,' said Jeremy James.

'You?' exclaimed the Reverend Cole.

'I know the lines,' said Jeremy James.

'It's true,' said Richard. 'He knows everybody's part.'

The Reverend Cole's watery eyes opened wide behind his glasses. It was as if he had suddenly seen a bright star over the High Street.

'Do you really dow the lides?' he asked.

Jeremy James recited some of the lines, and the Reverend Cole rubbed his hands like a shepherd on a cold winter's night.

'Try od the costube, thed,' he said.

The Virgin Mary's costume fitted Jeremy James perfectly.

'This is really quite rebarkable,' said the Reverend Cole. 'Truly the Lord works id bysterious ways.'

'Please, Mr Cole,' asked Jeremy James, 'will I be the shepherd as well?'

'Ah, do,' said the Reverend Cole. 'I thick I'd better play that part byself.'

The run-through went quite well. Jeremy James forgot his lines twice, and Trevor forgot his three times, and Richard accidentally bumped into the crib and sent baby Jesus flying across the platform, but otherwise there were no disasters.

The performance was due to start at three o'clock, and so all the actors had to be back by

111

half-past one, in order to leave time for make-up, last minute adjustments to costumes, and last minute adjustments to the Reverend Cole's prayers. To his relief, everyone came punctually, and all he had to pray for was the Lord's goodwill, which he knew he had already.

At five-to-three, the Reverend Cole announced to a packed church that as Sarah Goody had fallen ill, the part of the Virgin Mary had been taken over at the last minute by Jeremy James. The part of the shepherd would. . . um. . . be played by 'byself'.

Jeremy James peeped out into the church, and murmured to Richard that there were lots and lots of people there. Richard turned a little pale and said he was sure to forget some of his lines. Trevor turned even paler and said he was sure to forget all of his lines.

Jeremy James was dressed in a long costume with a shawl and a headscarf. He had red lips and red cheeks, and Mrs Grundy, who had made him up, had said he was the prettiest Virgin Mary she'd ever seen. (And Mrs Grundy had been making up Virgin Marys almost as long as the Reverend Cole had been directing them.) Jeremy James wasn't altogether sure that he *wanted* to be pretty, but on the whole he thought it better to be a pretty Virgin Mary than a cold shepherd.

The Reverend Cole came backstage.

'Right!' he whispered. 'Let's begid.'

When Jeremy James went out on to the platform with Peter Cutting, who was Joseph, he had quite a few lines to say straight away, and he said them all without making a single mistake. Then there was a passage while other people were speaking, and he had a look round the church. He spotted Mummy and Daddy and the twins sitting in the third row, and gave them a quick wave. Mummy waved back. (The Reverend Cole had told them not to wave at anyone, but the Reverend Cole was backstage, so he wouldn't know.)

Richard, as the inn-keeper, was very nervous, and when he forgot his words, Jeremy James whispered them to him.

'What?' said Richard.

Jeremy James said them a bit louder, and then Richard said, 'thank you' and repeated what Jeremy James had told him. But he couldn't remember the next words either, so Jeremy James had to tell him again.

The next scene was the shepherd's, and the Reverend Cole remembered all his words very well. But one or two people in the church giggled when he said, 'I thick I cad see a star shidig over Bethleheb.'

Trevor forgot his lines several times. But

nobody noticed because he spoke so softly that even Jeremy James could hardly hear him, although they were next to each other on the platform.

In spite of everything, the play was a great success, and there were no disasters at all. At the end everybody clapped, and there was an especially loud clap for the Virgin Mary, who smiled straight at Mummy and Daddy, who smiled back.

Then the Reverend Cole made a little speech, in which he congratulated all the children, said how hard they'd worked and what a pleasure it had been to produce the play, and he was now looking forward to producing one again next year. He finished by saying:

'I'd like to bake a special bedtion of Jereby Jabes who. . . ub. . . acted the Virgid Bary at just a few hours' dotice. Well dud. . . ub. . . Jereby Jabes.'

Then he let out a loud sneeze, and everybody said, 'Bless you.'

'Add bless you, too,' said the Reverend Cole.

David Henry Wilson

**The Fastest Gun Alive
and other night adventures** 95p

Melvin Woolaway and his friends live out their wildest fantasies in their dreams. Melvin, as 'Big Mel', goes gunning for the Headmaster! His friend plays in goal for England — with disastrous results! And there are many more hilarious adventures with the twelve classmates of Wimpleford Junior School.

Elephants Don't Sit on Cars £1.25

But it *was* an elephant Jeremy James saw sitting on Daddy's car — the car wasn't too happy about it.

Grown-ups in Jeremy James's experience live in a different world. Jeremy, a natural troublemaker, gets into some hilarious adventures with baby-sitters, burglars and elephants — and he has a *smashing* time in the supermarket.

Getting Rich With Jeremy James £1.25

Getting rich is just one of Jeremy James's problems in this hilarious sequel to *Elephants Don't Sit On Cars*. When he's not hunting for money, he's causing trouble for Daddy's car, Santa Claus's beard, and the vicar's sore bottom. But trouble gets its own back in the form of an aching tooth, a ghost in the bedroom, and a cow that isn't a cow — not to mention spoilt Timothy, who wins all the prizes.

David Henry Wilson

How to Stop a Train with One Finger £1.50

Jeremy James does it again! It's not every small boy who can stop a train with one finger in an effort to save his fellow passengers, cause laughter in the theatre, panic in the library or devastation in the darkroom. But Jeremy James can and does. With his irrepressible good nature, unquenchable curiosity and unique brand of logic, he tackles the adult world head on!

Beside the Sea With Jeremy James £1.25

When Jeremy James goes on holiday, trouble goes with him. Trouble with motorway policemen, with Mrs Gullich, their landlady, and her house of secrets, with a non-go, non-stop donkey – and especially with Timothy Smyth-Fortescue! But Warkin-on-Sea offers Jeremy James some success, too - when treasure hunting, foreign languages and life-saving make him a hero!

Maurice Dodd
Merrymole the Magnificent £1.50

From the creator of *The Perishers* comes the magnificent Merrymole, fighting the Woodland Council for the right to live in his amazing tree-top home. Determined *not* to live underground, Merrymole takes his case to the *people* and, aided by the likes of Michael O'Hare, Beetle, and Dan Hedgehog with his army of tramps, he faces the dreaded Major Frogge and his gang of cut-throats . . .

Susan Williams
A Year at Sheepfold Farm £2.50

Now collected together in one volume and in paperback for the first time, the *Sheepfold Farm* trilogy tells the story of a lowland shepherd's life and work through the eyes of Jack Evans, his wife Betty and their children Polly and Tim.

Susan Williams' delightful and informative story perfectly captures the atmosphere and activity of the changing seasons, and her own detailed illustrations are full of the magic of the countryside.

Meryl Doney
Goodnight Stories £1.25

A marvellous collection of stories from some of the world's best writers. Some sad stories, some happy stories, but all with a tale to tell. Goodnight and sweet dreams from giants, princes, wicked animals, good animals, and boys and girls from around the world.

Goodnight!

Frank Herrmann and George Him
All About the Giant Alexander £1.95

The Giant Alexander is sixty feet tall (as high as one telegraph pole on top of another). Over the years the adventures of this endearing, though rather fierce-looking giant, have given much pleasure to countless children all over the world.

Read all about how Alexander got the Lord Mayor of London out of a tight spot, what happened when the President summoned him to America, how he skated up the motorway to rescue a stolen elephant, and how he helped the fire brigade the night the circus came to town. And in case you wondered how he actually *became* a giant, the secret details are revealed for the first time (but you must promise not to tell anyone . . .)